Soul Prep

Train Your Senses, Fortify Your Mind

SHARON BOLAND

Published by Living Hope, Inc.
Living Hope, Inc., PO Box 2840, Cleveland, GA 30528, U.S.A.

First Edition, April 2013

Copyright © Sharon Boland, 2013
All rights reserved

Boland, Sharon.
Soul Prep : Train Your Senses, Fortify Your Mind. / Sharon Boland.

ISBN 978-1484807903

Set in Adobe Garamond
Design by Justin C. Boland

Without limiting the rights under copyright reserved above, no part of this publication may be reproduced, stored in or introduced into a retrieval system, or transmitted, in any form, or by any means (electronic, mechanical, photocopying, recording, or otherwise), without the prior written permission of both the copyright owner and the above publisher of this course.

PUBLISHER'S NOTE
The scanning, uploading, and distributing of this book via the Internet or via any other means without the permission of the publisher is illegal and punishable by law. Please purchase only authorized electronic editions, and do not participate in or encourage electronic piracy of copyrighted materials. Your support of the author's rights is appreciated.

Scripture taken from the HOLY BIBLE, NEW INTERNATIONAL VERSION®. Copyright © 1973, 1978, 1984, 2011 Biblica. Used by permission of Zondervan. All rights reserved. The "NIV" and "New International Version" trademarks are registered in the United States Patent and Trademark Office by Biblica. Use of either trademark requires the permission of Biblica.

Scriptures noted (NKJV) are taken from the The Holy Bible, New King James Version Copyright © 1982 by Thomas Nelson, Inc. Used by permission.

Table of Contents

Dedication 5
About the Author 6
Introduction 7
My Heart is Fixed 9
Wisdom 13
Faith 17
Strength In My Soul 21
God's Love 25
Trust 29
Fear 33
Just Let Go 37
Season and Purpose 39
Gathering A Few Sticks 43
Encourager 47
Worship 49
Praises 53
Do What is Right 55
Like-Minded 59
Sensory Therapy 63
Two 67
Hijacked by Emotions 69
The Hills 73

Under the Shadow 75
The Heart 79
God's Pursuit 81
Free Will 83
Why 87
Comfort 91
No Negotiating 95
Thanks 99
Enough's Enough 103
His Workmanship 107
Train Your Senses 111
God's Will 115
Hope Deferred 119
Make It Easy On Yourself 123
Enough Faith 127
Serve 131
God With Skin On Him 135
I Will Always Be Here For You 139
Love God Where You Are 143
Examine Yourself 147
Are You Ready? 151
Encouragement For Your Soul 155

Dedication

It is with deepest gratitude that I dedicate this book to ... My late grandmother, Opal Cook, who taught me how to love and serve with God's love through the example of her life. My mother, Billie Scroggins, who loves unconditionally, and has been my greatest support. She believed in me when I didn't believe in myself. She truly exemplifies Proverbs 31. My dad, Norman, who came alive when he learned the truth about the heart we give to God, Nancy Harmon, who taught me the power of a strong prayer life, and Loraine Daniel, who mentored me in God's Word and taught me how to study and teach it in a practical way making it applicable to life. Teresa Hurt, my BFF, who has been my most loyal friend and who tirelessly edited my work, and my son, Justin, whose talent in graphic design brought it all together.

About the Author

SHARON BOLAND has traveled throughout the United States evangelizing, speaking at conferences, was a soloist with Nancy Harmon Ministries, served as Vice President of the Apple of His Eye Ministries, and has been a frequent guest of the Love Special, TBN, Daystar and Cornerstone Television Network. She founded Loving Life Cancer Recovery in 1995, which is presently a part of Living Hope, Inc. She has served as Senior Pastor in Pennsylvania and Georgia.

Sharon's desire has been to empower people as she speaks God's Word with practical application, giving hope to those who are discouraged, disheartened, or disillusioned. Sharon is an ordained minister, gospel singer, a gifted and true servant of the Lord, with a genuine love for people that shows and communicates.

Introduction

Evil bombards our mind on a daily basis. It comes to render us powerless. It comes to pull us away from the safety, virtue and power of God's Word. It is important that we understand that evil comes to our mind. It is important that we understand God's Word as it pertains to how we overcome evil. Far too long, many Christians have aspired to serve God with an abstract relationship never understanding how we truly connect to Him. Scripture says, *"And you must love the LORD your God with all your heart, all your soul, all your mind, and all your strength." Mark 12:30*

Soul Prep is a simple, practical tool that will empower you as you learn how to fortify your mind. It will help you learn how to overcome the difficulties of life by making deliberate decisions resulting in a positive outcome. It will encourage you to trust God. It will help you see that you are here for the purpose of loving God and serving others with eternal reward. Every day we live, we are to strive to develop the character of Jesus Christ. It seems that much of our character development comes through our troubles. I pray that you will see, as never before, who you are in Him. You are of tremendous value to God and others. Let's begin this journey of Soul Preparation!

My Heart is Fixed

*"My heart is fixed, O God, my heart is fixed;
I will sing and give praise." Psalm 57:7*

Have you ever noticed how fickle people are? Too many are vacillating back and forth with what they believe. We are living in a generation that is gray; anything goes as long as it doesn't hurt anyone. The problem with that belief system is that someone is always hurt. God's Word has never changed, and it will never change. In fact, it says in Hebrews 13:8, *"Jesus Christ is the same yesterday, today and forever."* It really comes down to this ... either you believe His Word to be truth or you don't.

Let's look at these two words **heart** and **fixed** in this scripture.

There are two Hebrew words for **heart**:
1.) *lebab*, **the heart, the middle of something, the center, the physical heart in the chest, the blood pumping organ.**
2.) *leb*, **the deepest inmost part of you, inner or immaterial nature, seat of reason, emotions, understanding, the will, mind, passions, intellect.**

The Hebrew word for **fixed** is *kuwn*. It means **established, stable, firmly established, securely determined, be settled.**

The word **heart** David is talking about isn't the heart in your chest. It does nothing but pump blood throughout the circulatory system. There is nothing spiritual about the heart in your chest. It cannot reason or think. The **heart** David is talking about is the heart of **your mind, your will, your intellect,** that inmost part of you no one knows but God. David has determined that his heart (mind, his will) is firmly established as to whom he is serving. His mind is made up. No vacillating. No question. It is settled.

Proverbs 4:23 says, *"Keep your heart with all diligence, for out of it are the issues of life."* This simply means to guard and protect your mind because out of it flows the results of your life. This is something we must do.

In every chapter of this book, you will see over and over again one pattern of thought and purpose, and that is you must give your mind, your will, your intellect totally to God. There is one place the devil comes to tempt you, discourage you, and to defeat you. It is in your mind. We must fortify our minds by reading, understanding, and appropriating God's Word to our life. We must daily reinforce our faith in God through His Word and action. For when God has our will, our heart, He has all of us.

PRAYER

Father, today I have determined to give You all of me. I give You my heart. I desire for Your will to be mine. Give me a clean heart today to serve and please You. Give me a heart to serve others and to help them learn how to connect with You. Total surrender is what You desire, and I totally surrender to You today. Amen.

REFLECTION

Have you truly given your heart to God? Is your heart settled on serving the Lord?

_____
_____
_____
_____
_____
_____
_____

Wisdom

> *"How much better to get wisdom than gold, and understanding than silver!" Proverbs 16:16*

As we begin our journey into 'Soul Prep', wisdom is one of the first things we need to ask God for. Is your deepest desire to see as many people come to know Jesus through your life as possible? I know it is mine. For that to happen, we need God to give us wisdom. Oh, we have our plans and ideas, our schemes and dreams, but what about wisdom? We read how to be successful in magazines, books, how to become wealthy, prosperous people, but we seldom hear anything about true wealth, which is found in wisdom.

Wisdom coupled with understanding is better than gold and silver. Many would question that nowadays. To have wisdom and understanding is to truly be wealthy. Ultimately, as God gauges it, we will be successful if we can attain wisdom, common sense and integrity. We must pursue it, and in asking get understanding as to what is 'true riches'. I see 'true riches' as things which have eternal value.

The word **wisdom** comes from the Greek word *chokmaw* and it means **to be wise, in mind, word, or act; skillful, ethical, common sense.**

The word **understanding** comes from the Hebrew word *biynah* and it means **understanding, knowledge, and discernment.**

"He grants a treasure of common sense to the honest. He is a shield to those who walk with integrity. He guards the paths of the just and protects those who are faithful to him. Then you will understand what is right, just, and fair, and you will find the right way to go. For wisdom will enter your heart, and knowledge will fill you with joy. Wise choices will watch over you. Understanding will keep you safe." Proverbs 2:7-11

If there were ever a day in which we need wisdom, it is today. In all decisions we make, we need **wisdom** from God. To reach this generation for Christ, we need His guidance and understanding. Wisdom isn't something you're born with ... it is something we ask God for. In fact, I will go so far as to say that we cannot live successfully without it. As you begin this journey of 'Soul Prep', begin it with asking God for wisdom and understanding.

PRAYER

I know that true success is in those things that are eternal. I spend so much of my life striving to be successful here on the job, in school, raising a family, but if I could just wrap my brain around the fact that **success is beyond this life.** Help me to succeed in Your eyes. Give me wisdom to make right decisions. Help me to be a witness today to someone You bring across my path. Help me to **live out my faith.** Help me to be a **real** follower of **Christ Jesus.** Please Father, give me **wisdom.** Amen.

REFLECTION

Can you think of some things that have hindered your pursuit of wisdom and understanding? What is it that hinders your example of Christ to others?

_____
_____
_____
_____
_____
_____
_____

Faith

"I can do all things through Christ who strengthens me."
Philippians 4:13

Our failures as individuals generally lie not so much in our obstacles and problems as they do in our **lack of faith**. We've already **decided what is not going to work**, and **who's not going to respond**, and **what can't be done**. And somehow that soothes our conscience a little bit when we don't do anything because **"it wouldn't do any good anyhow"**. What a copout!

The Bible calls our life a *'race of faith'* in Hebrews 12:1-2. In racing terms, it is a marathon, not a 100 meter sprint. In fighting terms, it is a fifteen round contest and not a three-round bout. You've got to last to the end.

In I Timothy 6:12, it says *"Fight the good fight of faith for what we believe. Hold tightly to the eternal life that God has given you, which you have confessed so well before many witnesses."*

The Greek word for **fight** here is ***agonizomai***. We get our English words agonize and agony from its root. It literally means **to struggle with perseverance**.

Faith comes from the Greek word ***pistis***, and it means **belief with the predominate idea of trust (or confidence) whether in God or in Christ, springing from faith in the same**. It is belief in God, trust in God and pledging our fidelity to God **no matter what**.

We must aim to win the race and complete the course. We can do anything God calls us to do. Our courage is in knowing that He is with us.

 The word **strengthen** in Philippians 4:13 comes from the Greek word *endynamoo* and means *to be strong, endure with strength, strengthen, to receive strength, be strengthened, increase in strength.*

Paul didn't say "I have fought the fight of faith." He said, **"I have fought the good fight of faith."**
What is a good fight? It is one that WE WIN!

You cannot listen to all the voices of those who have said you won't make it or you are going to fail ... voices of discouragement. We must be strong in our faith. Thank God for the tenacity to persevere and trust Him! And the stubborn will to complete what He has called you to do.

The Lord's work has not always been done by the most educated, talented people, or even outgoing people. **But it has been done by people who believe in the power of God, who do what they can, relying on God to supply the rest. God wants to use you!**

PRAYER

Search me and forgive me if I have been apathetic and lazy concerning Your call on my life. You have called me to be a witness of Your love and to care for those who are hurting and don't know You. Forgive me Lord, and *help me to change. Help me to become bold in my faith* and witness of what You have done for me. Today, bring someone across my path to whom I can be a witness of Your love. Amen.

REFLECTION

What is the definition of faith? Are you living this faith out?

_____

_____

_____

_____

_____

_____

Strength In My Soul

"Bring my soul out of prison that I may praise your name; The righteous shall surround me, For you shall deal bountifully with me." Psalm 142:7

David's life was filled with one crisis after another. He had hostile armies chasing him; he was lied on to the point that people wanted him dead! At this particular time, scripture says that he was hiding in a cave! David had trouble. This is the same guy that as a teenager the prophet Samuel anointed to be king of Israel! I can just imagine the thoughts going through David's mind ... 'God, why am I here? The enemy is all around me, they want to kill me, and where are you? I guess the Prophet was wrong. I'm in this cave, and I'll probably die in this cave!' He was depressed. His soul was worn, tired and dull. Darkness shrouded his mind. In that moment he saw no hope. He was in a mental prison. But then he remembered the faithfulness of His God.

"In the day when I cried out, you answered me, and made me bold with strength in my soul." Psalm 138:3

The Hebrew word for **soul** is *nephesh*, and it means **soul, life, mind, passions, and emotions, activity of mind, will and character.**

The Hebrew word for **prison** is *cagar*, and it means **close up, shut up, give up, stop, shut**

> in self, a dark place.
>
> The Hebrew word for **praise** is *yadah*, and it means **to give thanks, to confess the name of God.**

Are you dealing with depression? Is your mind worn and dull? Does it feel like a dark cloud has shrouded your mind? When David was filled with this much anxiety, all he could think about was himself and his troubles. All he saw was the darkness and all he felt was hopelessness and aloneness. That is exactly where the enemy wants us, hopeless. A dear friend of mine, Nancy Harmon, gave one of the most interesting definitions of what depression is. She said that she was praying one day about depression because she didn't understand it. She asked God to show her what depression was and He said "depression is worship turned inward." If you are dealing with depression, this could make you instantly angry, but hear me out.

Anytime we begin to turn inward (feel sorry for ourselves), we are in trouble. When the problem becomes our main focus, that problem will be blown out of proportion. We will give it front and center of our thought life. It will consume us, and there will be no room for anything else. The only way David came out of depression was when he cried out to God and looked at his track record. God had given him power in his past to overcome his enemies. He gave him supernatural power to kill the lion, the bear, and the giant. He began to think about those things when he deliberately recalled the victories he had experienced. **HE CRIED OUT TO GOD, AND GOD GAVE HIM STRENGTH IN HIS SOUL (mind) TO BRING HIM OUT OF HIS MENTAL PRISON.** He came out of that mental prison when he began to **'yadah'**, confess the name of God and give thanks. He began to rehearse all that God had done for him and faith began to fortify his mind.

It is the same for us today. When we cry out to the Lord, confess our sin, confess the name of God, thank Him for His faithfulness, and give Him praise, **we will come out of our mental prison!** We have to change the pattern of our thinking and be renewed in the spirit/life of our mind. God will give us boldness and strength to move forward in victory!

Too often we are not compassionate towards those suffering depression. Perhaps it is because we really don't understand it. So let me interject this thought ... when crying out to God, applying His Word and trying to take captive the negative thoughts do not bring about the desired results ... **relief, victory** as it did for David, then it may be time to seek professional help. There may be a chemical imbalance that needs to be addressed. Do not be ashamed or embarrassed if you need to seek professional help. **IT DOES NOT MEAN YOU DON'T HAVE ENOUGH FAITH TO BE HEALED! IT DOES NOT MEAN YOU ARE NOT A GOOD CHRISTIAN.** It means there is something physically wrong. God loves you and is compassionate towards you. He gives doctors the wisdom and knowledge to help. Either way, there is **strength for your soul.** If you must seek out help, then pray and ask the Lord to lead you to the right counselor or physician.

PRAYER

Father, help me; forgive me for giving my problems so much energy and time. Bring my soul out of this mental prison that I might live life to the fullest. Bring my soul out of prison that I might praise Your name. You are faithful even in the middle of injustices, sorrow and disappointments. You are faithful, and I thank You and praise You. Amen.

REFLECTION

Are you depressed? Can you identify what is causing the depression? If so, what is it? Do you find relief when you dump the problem in God's lap? If not, then what should you do?

_____
_____
_____
_____
_____
_____
_____

God's Love

"Who shall separate us from the love of Christ? Shall trouble or hardship or persecution or famine or nakedness or danger or sword? ... neither height nor depth, nor anything else in all creation, will be able to separate us from the love of God that is in Christ Jesus our Lord."
Romans 8:35, 39

I had a precious friend who suffered deep depression and constant thoughts of suicide. Through the years, I used to wonder why she wouldn't get help. Then, I came up with what I believe are three very valid reasons as to the question **'why'** she wouldn't seek out help.

PRIDE – She had a brilliant mind. She knew more of the Word of God than most. She taught about the power of the God's Word that could change our lives. She created credos to live by that were effective, and in fact, so effective that they literally changed lives. Yet, she was unable to successfully live what she taught. She struggled with inner demons that tormented her mind. She was a beautiful woman outside and inside, but when this torment hit her she could become cruel and then go into depression for days at a time. God called me to walk with her, serve her, and love her, and I did just that many years. I must admit that I had no experience with anyone who suffered with mental illness. It was very difficult at times, but I always saw her well and whole. I believe God allowed me to see that picture to be able to continue the walk with her to the end of her life. When I say that pride was one issue what I mean is that she was so intelligent that at times her attitude was that she knew more than others. She had the answers of how to live life and didn't need help.

FEAR – At times when we would talk about her torment and I would mention to her about getting help, her first response was, **"What would people think? What would her peers think? What would those who had heard her teachings say?"** There is an old cliche in the church world "**Christians kill their wounded**". Isn't that sad? But some who call themselves Christians do exactly that. They judge and condemn the wounded and hurting. Well, to me people who do that are not true Christ followers.

SHAME – She felt ashamed that she couldn't get on top of her problem. She was ashamed that she couldn't make the Word of God work to the extent that she would never be troubled with it again. She absolutely believed what she taught with all of her heart. But she couldn't overcome the times rage would overtake her and then depression. She felt ashamed and that was another thing that kept her from seeking help. **We should never allow what others might think or say to keep us from seeking out help when it's needed.** During the latter years of my friend's life, the doctors gave her a low dosage of an antidepressant, and I have to tell you that it helped balance her out. She, for the first time, was able to function with a totally sound mind during the last years of her life. You see, she really did have a chemical imbalance and the medication helped her. Her last years were greater than her past. She touched more lives, I believe, more effectively in those years than in her past. God touched her and healed many past hurts in her life, and she was able to truly forgive. Many times Satan takes advantage of those who suffer with mental issues, and oh my goodness, do you ever need God's strength and help in dealing with it. But, He is faithful to be there to help us and strengthen us, to give us discernment, and to give us His love to keep fighting the fight. **Mental illness is the most difficult, confusing, complex, frustrating disease there is. It requires more strength, patience, tolerance, and forbearance than we humanly have and only God can give.**

My heart is saddened when I hear of people who love the Lord, and yet are overwhelmed by hopelessness in their minds and desperation drives them to the point of taking their own life. No, I don't understand it, **BUT GOD is full of mercy, and one thing we cannot judge is the heart of another.** Only God can do that. Today, you or someone you know may be dealing with mental illness. You may not know what to say or do, but I want to encourage you to just write a note telling them that you are praying for them and love them. Just a small act of kindness can mean so much. **Just show them God's love. What is God's love?** Our scripture on page 25, Romans 8:35, 39, describes love perfectly.

> **PRAYER**
> Heavenly Father, only You know the depths of the mind and heart. Only You know the hidden thoughts that torment and the accusations a mind can be bombarded with from the evil one. You are full of mercy and compassion. Your love is so far reaching that my finite mind cannot fully comprehend it. Help me not to judge or condemn that one who is hurting. Help me to turn over to You what I do not understand. Give me compassion and help me to love with Your love, which is unconditional, those who are

dealing with mental darkness. In the name of Jesus. Amen.

THOSE DEALING WITH MENTAL DARKNESS
I pray in the power of the name of Jesus Christ, that His Holy Spirit right now reaches into the hidden parts of your heart, and that He calms your troubled mind. I pray that your mind is filled with His peace, and that you will be comforted knowing that He loves you beyond what you are able to understand. I pray that you know He does not condemn you, and He is always as close as the name of His blessed son, Jesus. God's mercy is reaching to you right now to bring healing to every hurt, every pain. Amen.

REFLECTION
Are you or someone you know dealing with mental torment? After seeking God in prayer, have you found relief? If not, have you sought out a counselor or a physician to help you? Do not hesitate to seek out help.

_____
_____
_____
_____

Trust

"Trust in the Lord with all your heart; do not depend on your own understanding. Seek his will in all you do, and he will direct your paths." Proverbs 3:5, 6

"Blessed is the man who trusts in the Lord whose confidence is in Him." Jeremiah 17:7

I suppose, if we were honest, most all of us have a problem with trust. It is difficult to trust people. It may be because you have been disappointed in someone, or someone has lied to you or about you. That makes it hard to trust. And sometimes that goes right on over into our trust of and in God. Yet, God has never lied nor will He ever lie. **WE CAN TRUST HIM.**

 The word **trust** comes from the Hebrew word *batach,* and it means **to trust, to trust in, to be confident, to be bold, to be secure.**

It's so easy to put your trust in what you read in a newspaper or magazine or what you hear and see on television or other media than it is to put your faith and trust in God, whom you have not seen.

It takes a deliberate effort to believe in God. It takes a deliberate act of your will to believe the Word of God and to act on it before it can become a reality to your life. And your life will show the fruit of that deliberate faith and trust.

In our nation there is so much unrest. People are under so much stress. Truthfully, I don't know how they do life without God. There is only one thing that gives me strength to push forward and that is knowing that God is with me, God is in me, and God is for me. In my study of Proverbs 3:5, I have written a paraphrased version:

Be confident in the Lord with all your heart, mind, and will; do not depend on your own understanding. In all of your ways, recognize His authority, express gratitude, take notice of and recognize the genuine validity of who God is and He will make your way straight.

Today make a deliberate decision to trust in the Lord. You can trust Him. He will work the things out that concern you.

PRAYER
With all of my heart, I want to trust You. I know in the depths of my being that You have my best interest at heart. I have to admit that I don't always understand Your ways, but I know You love me and are concerned about everything that touches my life. Help me to push beyond my unbelief and doubts. Help me to fully trust You. I surrender my life, my fears, my dreams, and my hopes to You. I trust You with all of me and all that I hold dear. Use me, Father, to be a witness of Your love. Amen.

REFLECTION

Do you really believe the Bible is the Word of God? Do you really trust Him with all of your heart even though life is so confusing at times?

_____
_____
_____
_____
_____
_____
_____

Fear

"For God has not given us the spirit of fear, but of power and of love and of a sound mind." II Timothy 1:7

I remember years ago a man had murdered a woman in our neighborhood and 'fear' grabbed a hold of my mind. They hadn't caught him. I was so tormented by that fear of "what if he comes to my house", that I would get up, get the rifle, and walk the floor until the sun rose. I did that night after night. It wasn't long until I was just plain worn out! Finally, one night I thought, "I can't do this anymore. I'm just too tired." I put the gun by the bed and my Bible on my chest and said, "God, I'm tired of being afraid. I am going to trust you to protect me. I'm going to sleep!"

The Bible says that 'fear has torment' and it does. It was never God's intent that we live frightened, alarmed, and live in dread or terror. It is His heart that we live in peace though the world around us is in chaos. We can have a deep settled peace that even we don't fully understand when we make a decision to trust God.

The Greek word for **fear** is *deilia,* and it means **timidity, fearfulness, dread, terror, to be alarmed, cowardice.**

The Greek word for **power** is *dunamis,* and it means **miraculous power, ability, might.**

The Greek word for **love** is *agape,* and it

> means **affection, good will, benevolence, brotherly love.**
>
> The Greek word for **sound mind** is *sophronimos,* which is **self control, discipline.**

There are many things that cause the spirit of fear to come to our minds, BUT GOD hasn't given us the spirit of fear. Let's look at this scripture and words in a little more depth.

God has given us the ability to use self control and discipline to take our thoughts captive. He won't do that for us ... we do that. When we take control of our thoughts, we can then make a rational decision that is best for whatever the circumstance. In every situation we face, we need to settle in our mind that God is able to take care of everything that concerns us.

Nothing takes God by surprise. Faith, believing, and trusting God will overcome the spirit of fear. Again, it is a deliberate act of our will to trust Him.

PRAYER

God, I know You haven't given me the spirit of fear. You don't want me to allow it to control my life. I choose today to trust You. Whenever I'm afraid, I WILL trust in You, my God. Thank You for Your peace. Amen.

REFLECTION

What do you fear? Do you understand that fear is a spirit? Do you believe that it is God's will for you to have peace of mind?

Just Let Go

"Around midnight, Paul and Silas were praying and singing hymns to God, and the other prisoners were listening." Acts 16:25

I love a story that I read about a little boy who went to jump on the bumper of his dad's truck in order to get a short ride across the yard. The dad didn't see him, and the little boy slid down and was being dragged for several yards before his dad heard him screaming. The father ran around behind the truck where his son was still holding on to the bumper. He saw the boy was okay, just a little scratched up on his knees and legs. His dad just had to ask the obvious question, "Son, why didn't you just let go?"

God must look at us at times and wonder '*Why don't you just let go?*' There are many things we are powerless over. Yet, we keep hanging on to them, fretting about them, losing sleep over them, stressing over them. **If we would make a decision to trust God** and **'just let go'**, **He is well able to take care of what concerns us.**

It takes **faith** to *let go* and *trust* God when *stuff* happens … especially things we have no control over. But once we have prayed and put our problems in God's capable hands, what else is there to do but praise Him?

Paul and Silas were praying and praising God while being beaten and placed in prison over something they were not guilty of and yet, they learned the secret to overcoming the *stuff* they had no power over. They trusted in their God. They could have complained, sulked, become bitter, and hated God. But instead, they chose to praise God in spite of their trouble. They deliberately chose to "let go" of the injustices. They chose to trust God and praise Him. In doing so, the scripture says the other prisoners believed in Christ!

People are watching us. They are watching to see how we handle stress, injustices, and heartache. Are we living in such a way that they see the character of Jesus in us? The apostle Paul said that he died daily to attain this kind of character. Through his life he was able to say, *"Follow me as I follow Christ."* Oh how I want my life to exude this kind of faith and trust in God that others desire to emulate.

PRAYER

I don't know why I waste so much precious time on things I have no power over. I don't understand why I wait so long to turn it over to You. Help me to quickly *let go* of the *stuff* that weighs me down. I love You and thank You for helping me change. Amen.

REFLECTION

What do you need to *let go* of? Do you trust God enough to *just let go*?

_____

_____

_____

_____

_____

_____

Season and Purpose

"To everything there is a season, and a time for every purpose under heaven." Ecclesiastes 3:1

Everything God made was created with a specific design, purpose, and function. It is true of the animal and plant kingdoms, and it is true about you. You were not born simply to occupy space, eat food, poop, sleep, and get up to start the same old routine the next day. NO! You have a God given *purpose*.

People wander aimlessly from relationship to relationship, job to job, alcohol to drugs, trying to fill a vacuum deep inside their soul when they don't know Jesus. Even some Christians have these troubles when they haven't discovered their purpose. That vacuum is only filled when you step into God's will and have the satisfaction of knowing that you're right smack dab in the middle of His plan for your life.

> **Word Truth**
>
> The Hebrew word for **season** is *zman*, and it means **a time, an appointed occasion.**
>
> The Hebrew word for **purpose** is *chephets*, and it means **a valuable thing, a matter (as something in mind), a pursuit, a desire.**

To everything there is a season. There is a time to laugh, a time to cry, a time to live, a time to die, a time to be still, and a time to go. A season is an appointed period of time. It doesn't last forever. It may seem like it does, but thank God when we are in the middle of trouble we can know that it will pass, and if we keep our faith in God, we will come through it in victory!

There is a reason you are here on this earth. A reason you are where you are right now. God wants you to know that He has a purpose for you. He has called you to fulfill the great commission. Do you know what that means? It means that He has called you to share Jesus to those around you. He has called you to *'live the life'* that pleases Him in front of your friends, family and strangers.

Seek God. Ask Him how you can better fulfill your purpose. Even right now where you are God has a purpose. In any season we are in, God is working to perfect the love and character of His Son, Jesus, in us. He is working in you right now whether you are in a painful season or a season of joy. God is working His purpose in you. Don't fret, but trust Him even through the tears. Choose to love Him, choose to move forward.

PRAYER

Father, sometimes it seems like I'm just taking up space. I don't want to just live my life. I want to live the life YOU intend for me. Show me YOUR way. Speak to my mind and spirit and I will do what You place in front of me to do. I want to follow You. Change me … lead me. Amen.

REFLECTION

Are you in a season of doubt? Are you in a season of uncertainty? Do you realize that you have been given the power to come through this season with victory? How can you overcome?

Gathering A Few Sticks

"As surely as the Lord your God lives', she replied, 'I don't have any bread, only a handful of flour in a jar and a little oil in a jug. I am gathering a few sticks to take home and make a meal for myself and my son that we may eat it and die.'" I Kings 17:12

This is the story of the widow and her son. As far as this woman was concerned, she was saying "*it's over*." Yet, here are the next words Elijah said to her in verse 13 ... "***don't be afraid***". In other words, 'God has everything under control. It's going to be alright.' (my paraphrased version)

Isn't it true that when things get tough, we naturally shift into survival mode? The thought of prosperity was long gone from this woman. There was no hope! Yet, her breakthrough was just an ***obedient act*** away.

Your breakthrough may be a phone call away, a chance meeting, a letter, or an idea away. The word that Elijah spoke to that woman, Moses spoke to the Israelites. ***"Fear not, for I am with you, be not dismayed for I am your God." Isaiah 41:10***

> **Word Truth**
>
> The word **dismayed** means **to cause to lose courage or resolution or to un-nerve by arousing fear.** It means that **one is disconcerted and at a loss as to how to deal with something, it stresses a reaction of horror, disheartening, frightening in a venture requiring courage**.

> The words **fear not** come from the Hebrew word *yare*, and it means **frightened, afraid, and dread.**

This widow was afraid that she and her son were going to die. But God sent Elijah by to give her a message. That message was one of hope through obedience. It was a message that made no sense. She was telling him that she was preparing their last meal. And Elijah said, **"I want that"**. At that moment, she had a decision to make. A last meal for her son or feed the prophet? She decided to believe the message of Elijah for a continued provision, and she obeyed his request. And God was faithful to the message she was given.

Fear not is mentioned 365 times throughout the Bible. Every day you awake and deal with the problems of that day, the Lord would say to you, **"FEAR NOT, DON'T BE AFRAID."**

Tough times come to prove that God is faithful. And they will make you resilient and hopeful, not in your own strength, ideas or efforts, *but in God*. Things may look gloomy today, but *keep pushing forward* in your trust and faith in God's ability to work them out in *His time, His way, for your good.*

PRAYER

Father, I have found myself dismayed quite a bit lately, vacillating back and forth in my faith. I realize how human I am and how that I haven't reached that place of faith I so desire. I need Your help. I thank You for Your patience and love. And I even thank You for allowing circumstances to come into my life to help me grow in my faith and trust in You. Use me today, to help another with this same struggle. Amen.

REFLECTION

Have you been dismayed? Have you felt the circumstances of life overwhelming you? What are they? Are you being obedient to take what you have for God to use?

Encourager

"God has given each of us the ability to do certain things well. So if God has given you the ability to prophesy, speak out when you have faith that God is speaking through you. If your gift is serving others, serve them well. If you are a teacher, do a good job of teaching. If your gift is to encourage others, do it! If you have money, share it generously. If God has given you leadership ability, take the responsibility seriously. And if you have a gift for showing kindness to others, do it gladly. Don't just pretend that you love others. Really love them. Hate what is wrong. Stand on the side of the good. Love each other with genuine affection, and take delight in honoring each other." Romans 12:6-10

There is a man in the New Testament in Acts 4 by the name of Barnabas. His name literally means **'Son of encouragement'**. Pretty neat name, huh? People like to be around people who encourage them.

Word Truth

The root meaning of the word *encourage* simply means **to put courage in**, it means **the imputing or infusion of power** or **advice or inspiration that makes another person perform better**. Wow! That's good.

There are times in our lives when we feel low, unappreciated, tired, all pooped out, discouraged, drained of courage. Sometimes it's a crisis or just being spent. It can be sickness or hateful words that have been spoken. *To encourage is to do the direct opposite.*

Barnabas saw people through God's eyes. He always saw them through grace. He was generous and kind. He just loved doing good. We should think of ways to encourage one another to outbursts of love and good deeds. That is a true encourager.

PRAYER

Father, help me to operate in the gifts You have given me. Today, I ask You to help me be an encourager to those I meet. Help me to show love and acts of kindness that would cause others to push forward in the same way. Thank You, Father. Amen.

REFLECTION

How do you view people? Do you see them through God's eyes? Are you an encourager? Who do you know that needs encouraging?

_____
_____
_____
_____
_____
_____
_____

Worship

"But the time is coming and is already here when true worshippers will worship the Father in spirit and in truth. The Father is looking for anyone who will worship him that way. For God is Spirit, so those who worship him must worship in spirit and in truth." John 4:23, 24

What does it mean to worship God in **spirit** and in **truth**?

Word Truth

The word **spirit** comes from the Greek word *pneuma,* and it means **breath, the rational soul, mental disposition, and life.**

The Greek word for **truth** is *aletheia,* and it means **unclosedness, unconcealedness, disclosure or truth.** The literal meaning of the word *aletheia* is **the state of not being hidden; the state of being evident, and it also implies sincerity, as well as factuality or reality.**

When scripture says that we are to worship God in spirit and in truth, it simply means **we are to show true worship by the way we live.**

True worship isn't just singing songs to God, but something more important than our singing is living our lives in such a way that pleases God. **How are you living**

your life? What do people see when they are around you? Does your life exemplify your love for God?

You can be completely correct in your beliefs, yet fail to express your praise towards God who is so wonderful. Our worship must be based on truth and it should engage our intellect. Yet, worship also engages the affections, the mind and the emotions. Think about that.

People express their emotions at weddings, sports games, and political rallies. But, if they express emotions at church, they are labeled fanatics. Yet, the Bible encourages us to openly express our worship and praise to God. If we can act like fools at sports games, how much more should we emote in expressing our love, adoration and worship for Jesus Christ who gave his life to save us from eternal damnation! Did we deserve His love? I think not, yet He loves us! To the world we look foolish, but we make the heart of God happy when we worship Him in spirit and truth.

PRAYER

I love you and thank you for loving me. I know I have so far to go, but from the depths of my heart I want to love you and worship you in spirit and truth. I desire to live out my life in such a way that it makes you happy. Lord, I love you and I worship you, you are worthy to be praised. You are worthy. Amen.

REFLECTION

Are you really a *true worshipper*? How do you need to live to be a true worshipper of God?

_____
_____
_____
_____
_____
_____
_____

Praises

"God inhabits the praises of His people." Psalms 22:3

When an unbeliever comes into an anointed worship service, it can dramatically impact their life. They will be spiritually touched by seeing and hearing God's people in loving communion with the Lord.

When someone who is hurting walks into the atmosphere of sincere worship, it can be as an ointment soothing their pain. That is why it is so important that when worship is happening that we bring our thoughts captive, closing out anything that would distract us, or making sure that we are respectful during worship as to not be a distraction to others.

> **Word Truth**
>
> The word **inhabits** comes from the Hebrew word *yasha* which means God **dwells, occupies, resides, abides, sits, remains** where His people praise Him.
>
> **Praise** comes from the Hebrew word *tahillah*, and it means **praise, song** or **hymn of praise, adoration, renown, fame, glory of God**.

The Holy Spirit does more to meet our needs during praise and worship than any other time. So let me encourage you to forget about yourself, your inhibitions and concentrate on Jesus, and praise Him for all that He has done and is doing for you.

Right now, begin to think about things He has done for

you and praise Him. Begin to sing, dance, lift your hands, and just thank Him. Let's make God famous with our praise!

PRAYER

Father, I don't want to ask you for anything today. I just want to thank you for who you are in my life. Thank you for loving me when I was unlovable. Thank you for sending your Son to rescue me from my sinful self. Thank you for giving me a hope that is beyond this life. Thank you for your Holy Spirit that guides and teaches me your ways. Thank you for using my life as a living witness of your power. I praise you for just being who you are … Master, Lord, and Savior of my life. Amen.

REFLECTION

Does God inhabit your praise? What has He done for you that would cause you to praise Him?

_____
_____
_____
_____
_____
_____

Do What is Right

*"I have hidden your word in my heart,
that I might not sin against you." Psalms 119:11*

I love the story of how many years ago people would order large, beautiful statues made in Italy and ship them all over the world. Once in a while, the handlers, while packing the statues, would accidentally hit a nose, an arm or hand, and they would break off. Some of them did not have integrity, and they would take wax and put the broken piece back on, and you couldn't tell by the naked eye that anything was wrong until it sat in the sun a while. And then when the sun would beam down on it, the part that was inferior would fall off.

They had to come up with a plan to prove their work was genuine, and they began to tag their merchandise with the artist's name after the word 'Sincere'.

> **Word Truth**
>
> Sincere comes from two Latin words. The first is **sine** which means without, and the second one is **cera**, which means wax, without wax. Sincere means genuine as tested by the sun.

Wow! When the heat is on, the genuine stands the test.

*"May integrity and honesty protect me,
for I put my hope in You." Psalm 25:21*

"The godly walk in integrity; blessed are the children who follow them." Proverbs 20:7

Integrity is knowing the difference between right and wrong and making the decision to do what is right. Young, middle aged or old, daily we are tempted to compromise our integrity, our morals and our principles. In fact, we are living in a generation where what was wrong is now right, and what was right is now wrong morally. BUT, that does not change God's Word and standard. Sin is still sin. Wrong, according to God's Word, is still wrong. So, we are challenged to keep our integrity in tact, and we can do that by practicing God's Word in our daily life situations and do what is right. Will you stand the heat?

PRAYER

Father, every day I am tempted to compromise my walk with You. Every day evil comes to my mind to pull me away from Your truth. Give me the fortitude and strength to do what is right. Help me by the power of Your Holy Spirit to never compromise my life. I know that when I am obedient to Your word, I can expect You to take my back and protect me. Thank You for Your mercy. Amen.

REFLECTION

Are there things that you have been contending with that have caused you to compromise your walk with God? If so, what? What do you need to do about them?

_____
_____
_____
_____
_____
_____
_____

Like-Minded

"Therefore if there is any consolation in Christ, if any comfort of love, if any fellowship of the Spirit, if any affection and mercy, fulfill my joy by being like-minded, having the same love, being of one accord, of one mind. Let nothing be done through selfish ambition or conceit, but in lowliness of mind let each esteem others better than himself. Let each of you look out not only for his own interests, but also for the interests of others. Let this mind be in you which was also in Christ Jesus."
Philippians 2:1-5

Can you imagine being with a group of people whose minds are in agreement? All of us having one goal, one desire, God's unconditional love, being of one accord (of one mind), rather than seeking our own glory and pursuing our own agenda? The servant of God is concerned about one thing and that is **HONORING THE LORD**. The true servant of God doesn't care if they get the credit as long as God is honored and glorified through their lives. Today, let's be true servants!

> **Word Truth**
>
> The Greek word for **like-minded** is ***phroneo,*** and it means **to have understanding, be wise, to think, to have an opinion of one's self, think of one's self, to be modest, not let one's opinion (though just) of himself exceed**

the bounds of modesty, to think or judge what one's opinion is, to be of the same mind i.e. agreed together, cherish the same views, be harmonious.

The Greek word for **love** is *agape,* and it means **brotherly love, affection, good will, love, benevolence.**

The Greek word for **one accord** is *sumpsuchos.* This word is made up of two words: *sum* (**together with**) and *psuchos* (**soul, self, inner life, or the seat of the feelings, desires, and affections**). So, the **word refers to being united in spirit, one in Christ in all desires.**

PRAYER

Father, I want to be a true servant bringing You glory and honor by how I love my brothers and sisters. Give me a generous heart to help the poor, feed the hungry, visit the sick, help the widows and orphans, give of my substance, because You have given so much to me. Let me see those in need through Your eyes. Change me, please use me. Amen.

REFLECTION

What must you do to become "*like-minded*" with Christ?

_____
_____
_____
_____
_____
_____
_____

Sensory Therapy

"Peace I leave with you, my peace I give to you: not as the world gives, give I to you. Let not your heart be troubled, neither let it be afraid." John 14:27

There is a skin care product that I saw in Macy's. It is by **Origins** called **Sensory Therapy**. This certain product is called *Peace of Mind* lotion. Here is how they advertise it … "*When the world closes in on you and your head feels a size too small, apply just two dabs of Origins mind-clearing formula on the back of your neck, temples and earlobes. You'll feel a tingling sensation as pressure, tension and tightness begin to melt away.*" **OH MY WORD!** If that were true, I would be slathering that stuff all over my body. They wouldn't be able to keep it in the stores!

Then I found *Peace of Mind* mints. Here is how they advertise them … "*When you're having a stressful day, just pop one of these mind clearing mints into your mouth and feel your troubles melt away.*" If that were true, I'd be popping those peace mints 24/7! HELP US ALL!

There is only way to obtain true **'Peace of Mind'**, and that is through surrendering our lives to Jesus Christ. It is through Him, in Him, because of Him that we can have a peace in our minds in spite of hardships, pain, sorrow and losses. It is the *peace of God*. Jesus is our hope, Jesus is our strength, and Jesus is our peace. There is none without Him.

> **Word Truth**
>
> The word **peace** in the Greek is *eirene,* and it means **a state of tranquility, security, safety, prosperity, the Messiah's peace, the way that leads to peace** (salvation) **of Christianity, the tranquil state of a soul assured of its salvation through Christ, and so fearing nothing from God and content with its earthly lot, of whatsoever sort that is.**

You can't purchase this *peace*. It was already purchased for you 2000 years ago. Do you need peace today? A pill won't give it, a drink won't give it, a new love can't give it, and you can't find it in things. All of that is temporary. But, if you need lasting peace, I challenge you to go to Jesus with your need. He left ***His peace*** for you.

PRAYER

You know, Lord, I don't know when I will really learn that I can't bring about peace in my mind and life without You. I waste so much time trying to do it within myself, and I have to admit that I can't. I need You more than I can even express. I accept this peace right now that You left for me, and I thank You, Jesus, for loving me so much and caring. Your word is life to me. I love You. Amen.

REFLECTION

Do you have "peace of mind?" What is true peace of mind? Where can you find it?

_____
_____
_____
_____
_____
_____
_____
_____

Two

"Two are better than one, because they have a good reward for their labor." Ecclesiastes 4:9

I wish I knew who wrote this, but I don't. It's so good.

Alone we are a stone, together we are a temple.
Alone we are a member, together we are a body.
Alone we are a soldier, together we are an army.

Oh, the power of unity. God never intended for us to be alone. We can do so much more when there is another sharing the load. When one falls, the other can pick him up. When one is cold, the other can keep him warm. When one is weak, another can join him and they are strong. We need one another.

If we were to be honest, we would probably rather handle things ourselves. And, maybe for the most part, we can. But God created a need within all of us for fellowship. When we accept Jesus as Lord of our lives, we are engrafted into His family, and we become brothers and sisters spiritually. We are here to help one another. We are here to love one another. We are here on this planet to care for one another. We are here to pull our resources together to take the gospel of Jesus to those who are lost.

PRAYER

Dear Lord, honestly I don't want to have to

need anyone. I would rather just handle things myself. Yes, that's me ... *the all sufficient one.* You know me well. You created me. I do have to admit that it's so much easier when there is someone to share life's journey with. It is so wonderful to have brothers and sisters of like faith. Thank You for my precious brothers and sisters. Thank You for my family You have given to me that is eternal. Help me to carry my end of the load, to make it easier for those whom You desire me to walk with on this journey called life. I love You. Amen.

REFLECTION

Do you have a special friend, one that is there to walk with you through the stuff of life? If not, then can you be·one?

_____

_____

_____

_____

_____

_____

Hijacked by Emotions

"As a person thinks in his heart, so is he." Proverbs 23:7

Have you ever had a day when your emotions hijacked you? You resisted, you fought it, tried to distract yourself from the feelings, but they took over the entire day, eventually dumping you, exhausted into bed like a rung out dish rag!

Feelings appear to be **so arbitrary.** *"I can't help it, I just feel this way."* **So mysterious.** *"I have no idea why I feel this way."* **So irresistible.** *"There was nothing I could do to stop the feeling"*. **So powerful.** *"I was totally taken over by feeling the feeling."* **So paralyzing.** *"I was overwhelmed, immobilized by the feeling"*. We all have to deal with feelings. **What makes us feel what we feel?**

The answer is in the Scripture above, ***Proverbs 23:7, "As a person THINKS in his heart, so is he."*** There you have it, plain and simple. Our **thoughts** create **our internal experiences**, the things we call **feelings** and **emotions**. Feelings aren't caused by other people, circumstances, events or the devil. And they don't just come out of nowhere and attack you. They are **logical responses** to your **thoughts**. It's not the **sad event** that makes you **feel sad**. It's your **thoughts** about the **sad event** that makes you **feel** sad. It's not the **frightening event** that makes you feel **fear**, it's the **fearful thoughts** you think about the event that makes you **feel fear.**

It is **your thoughts alone that produce your feelings**.

Nobody <u>makes</u> you feel anything. <u>You do that by your own thoughts.</u>

I love this quote by Zig Ziglar, "***It's time to get a check up from the neck up to eliminate stinkin' thinkin'!***"

God has given you the power of free will. I love Loraine Daniel's credo, *"No one can make you feel badly about yourself without your permission."*

No one can make you feel mad, sad, hateful, angry, glad or any other emotion without your permission. God has given us the ability to discipline our thought life. We don't have to be hijacked by emotions.

PRAYER

Father, I have given too much power away to my life by giving into my feelings. Help me to bring my thoughts captive to Your Word. I see today that You have blessed me with the ability to control my thoughts. That is something I must do. Help me to do it, Holy Spirit. Help me to celebrate this day because it is all I really have. Yesterday is gone and tomorrow isn't here yet. You have known my past, You know today, and You know tomorrow. I am going to trust You. Help me be strong in my faith in You so that I can help someone today struggling. I love You. Amen.

REFLECTION

What are you thinking? How are your thoughts affecting your emotions? What can you do about them?

The Hills

"I will lift up my eyes unto the hills from whence comes my help; my help comes from the Lord who made heaven and earth." Psalms 121:1, 2

There is nothing more beautiful than the fall of the year in Georgia. There are rolling hills with the most beautiful array of colors. There is every shade of orange, yellow, red, purple, green, brown. It's just beautiful and so serene.

When I lift up my eyes and look at the hills, it always reminds me of this Scripture. As I look at the hills, I see the majesty of an awesome God, a God of all seasons, a God for all seasons. Nothing takes Him by surprise. We have a God, a Papa God, who is mindful of everything that concerns us. You may not feel that He is even near right now, but He is. And He is as close as the mention of His name, Jesus.

> **Word Truth**
> The word **eyes** in this scripture comes from the Hebrew word ***ayin***, and it means **physical eye, as showing mental qualities, of mental and spiritual faculties**.

With our physical eyes, we can see the magnificence of God's creative power. The psalmist, with a deliberate act of his will (mental faculties) recognized where He received His help. His help came from the Lord. His need was spiritual. It is no different for us today. We must deliberately recognize where our help comes from. Our need is spiritual. Our help is spiritual. It comes from the Lord.

If you are struggling today, lift up your eyes to the hills and be reminded that Your Father is right here to help you, to strengthen you, and to comfort you. He is aware of you today, and He loves you with an everlasting love. He is eager to help you.

PRAYER

Thank You, Father, for Your Word that sustains me when life around me feels really shaky. When I look at the hills today, I will be reminded of Your love, power and care for me. I am in awe to think that You really care about me. Help me to push beyond my self to see the need of another that I can share this word with and encourage them to not give up. I love You, Amen.

REFLECTION

There are times that we must encourage ourselves in the Lord. Is this a deliberate act? How do you encourage yourself in the Lord?

_____
_____
_____
_____
_____
_____
_____

Under the Shadow

"He that dwells in the secret place of the Most High, shall abide under the shadow of the almighty."
Psalm 91:1

I love to break down words, and I want to break this Scripture down for you today.

Word Truth

The word **dwells** comes from the Hebrew word *yashab,* and it means **to dwell, remain, sit abide, to stay.**

The words **secret place** come from the Hebrew word *cethar,* and it means **hidden, shelter, protection,** and **defense.**

The words **of the most High** come from the Hebrew word *elyown,* and it means **name of God, Highest.**

The words **shall abide** come from the Hebrew word *luwm,* and it means **to cause to rest, to dwell, abide, to lodge.**

The words **under the shadow** come from the Hebrew word *tsel,* and it means **protection, defense, shade.**

The words **of the Almighty** come from the Hebrew word *shaddy,* and it means **Almighty, most powerful God.**

Here is my paraphrased version:

If I abide in the protection of the Most High, I will find rest and be safe by the ALL-POWERFUL, INVINCIBLE, SUPREME, OMNIPOTENT God!

WOW! It looks to me like we're covered quite well **IF** we remain in Him. **How do we remain or abide or stay in that shelter?** We do it by *reading His Word, obeying His Word*, and *spending time talking to Him* (prayer), *worshipping Him, praising Him, loving Him.* He abides with us! He stays with us! He is our protection and defense. He will cause us to rest in His shadow because **He is the Almighty, Most Powerful God!** And we have another benefit ... **He is our Father!** Today let's rest in this Scripture. Accept that He loves you because you are very precious to Him. We are never alone! Thank you Jesus!

PRAYER

Father, Your words they comfort me. Your words bring me security in a world where nothing is secure. You are great! You are the Almighty God, the Most Powerful God and yet, You are the most loving, caring, Father... My Father, I love You. Amen.

REFLECTION

Do you long for that intimate fellowship with God? He longs for that with you. What are you doing to create that special time with God?

_____
_____
_____
_____
_____
_____
_____

The Heart

"For it is with the heart that you believe."
Romans 10:10

It always has amazed me how that we Christians want to compartmentalize and put God in the heart in our chest (the *viscera* section). The viscera area is the place where waste goes. We sometimes insult God with our ignorance. I suppose that the heart is romanticized, but it then becomes abstract trying to connect with God. What happens if you were to have a heart transplant? Where does Jesus go? The **heart** the Bible talks about is the **heart of your mind, your will, where you think, reason, analyze, interpret, and form conclusions.** The heart is where we make the decision to believe in God or not believe. What you believe determines what you become. Below is the proof.

> **Word Truth**
>
> The word **heart** comes from the Hebrew word *leb,* and it means **the mind, the will, the intellect, the center, core.**
>
> In the Greek, the word for **heart** is *kardia*, and it has two meanings. 1.) It is the **physical heart in the chest that pumps blood.** 2.) It is the **mind, will, emotions, understanding.**

YOU THINK WHAT YOU THINK BECAUSE YOU BELIEVE WHAT YOU BELIEVE.

Christian or sinner, your life and future are controlled by what you believe, even when what you believe is untrue. *A lie is as powerful as the truth, if you believe it to be true.* You may have an IQ of a genius, but if you believe you are stupid, your life will be dictated by that belief. What your heart believes, your mind cannot help but think!

YOU have the power to maximize your God given potential in every area of your life and overcome feelings of inadequacy, anxiety, depression, failure, victimization, inferiority, and intimidation.

The heart that God is talking about is the heart of the mind. It is your will.

PRAYER

God, I give my heart, my will to You today. You have all of me. Help me use discipline in my thinking. Help me to be cautious in what I allow to go into my mind. By the power of Your Holy Spirit, teach me all that is true and help me make good concrete decisions according to Your plan for my life. I believe in You, and I love You. Amen.

REFLECTION

Where is the heart you give to God? Have you given God your heart?

_____

_____

_____

_____

God's Pursuit

"I am sure that God, who began the good work within you, will continue His work until it is finally finished on that day when Christ Jesus comes back again."
Philippians 1:6

Do you ever feel that you are trying so hard to pursue God and things that are right and good in His eyes? Do you ever feel exhausted trying so hard to please Him, to gain favor with Him? Have you ever felt that the more you try the less you succeed? I'm sure all of us have felt like failures in our pursuit of God at one time or another.

Have you ever thought about God's constant pursuit of you? It's true. God is ever in pursuit of you. He is constantly, by the power of the Holy Spirit, working to perfect the love of His Son, Jesus, in each of us. That's a little overwhelming, isn't it? Just to think that God, the awesome, omnipotent God, the creator of the universe God, is so mindful of us that He is in pursuit of us, working His will and good pleasure in us! Wow! That's hard to wrap your mind around, but it is true. It is why He sent Jesus and why Jesus came in the form of man to earth.

Have you ever thought about the fact that Jesus came to earth of His own free will for two reasons?
    1.) His love for the Father.
    2.) His love for us.

Jesus came to show us how we are to act, live, and please God. He showed us how to truly love, forgive and overcome the hardships in this life. His example is perfect, and we are to follow it.

It's hard to imagine God a man, and yet, that is what He became. He became human to understand our emotions, fears, and struggles. And He overcame them all to prove to us that we could overcome. We overcome through the power of **His Spirit, His example and our obedience to God's Word. God is in pursuit of you, and He will not stop until we draw our last breath. He loves you that much!**

PRAYER

Father, thank You for loving me so much that You sent Jesus to show me that I can overcome the difficulties in this life. Jesus, thank You for loving our Father and *me* so much that You chose to come to understand my feelings of weakness, my pain, sorrow, joys, inadequacies, and my fears. Thank You for not giving up on me. Thank You for Your compassion towards me and the grace that You have given to see me through to the end. I love You so much. Amen.

REFLECTION

Do you have a difficult time believing that God is in pursuit of you? Do you believe He has something good in mind for you? If so, why?

_____

_____

_____

Free Will

"Today I have given you the choice between life and death, between blessings and curses. I call on heaven and earth to witness the choice you make. Oh that you would choose life, that you and your descendants might live!" Deuteronomy 30:19

I was thinking today of free will. God could have forced us to worship Him, but He didn't. We could have been slaves under the hand of an angry God, but we're not. God loved us so much that He gave us the gift of **free will (choice)**. Free will is the most amazing gift.

Every day we are faced with decisions. Some decisions are easy, some are obvious, some difficult, but they all come with **consequences,** either **good** or **bad**. When we make a decision, we are exercising the power of **free will**, a power we all have, yet must learn to use wisely.

We have the power to serve God or to reject Him. That is our choice. The decisions of God's people are so critical to their future, their children's future, and the nation's future. We are experiencing the ramification of poor choices in our nation now. It's choice, not chance, that determines our destiny. God is for us, the devil is against us, but we are the ones that will decide whom we will serve ... thus **free will**.

A good example of free will is in the Old Testament about a man named Moses. He was raised in the palace of the king, but chose to go with the God of his mother.

"He chose to share the oppression of God's people instead of enjoying the fleeting pleasures of sin. He thought it was better to suffer for the sake of the Messiah than to own the treasures of Egypt, for he was looking ahead to the great reward that God would give him." Hebrews 11:25, 26

Today will be full of decisions. We have the power to make the right ones that will bring peace, or we can be selfish, giving no thought of the pain it will cause others. Either way, we will experience the ramifications of those decisions. Choose Christ, love, peace, and hope!

PRAYER
Father, I choose You! I choose to do right and to try with all my heart to be obedient to Your Word. I choose life! I choose to walk in peace, even when evil comes against me. But I need Your help. I need Your guidance. I need Your wisdom. I love You with my life. You really are the love of my life. You are the hope that I cling to. You mean more than this world and everything in it to me. Thank You for the gift of free will. Amen.

REFLECTION

What do you choose today? You can be happy or sad, hateful or loving? Will you show kindness or vindictiveness? It's your choice. What will it be?

Why

"And we know that God causes everything to work together for the good of those who love God and are called according to His purpose for them." Romans 8:28

This scripture is a real challenge when we ponder the *'everything works together for the good'.* During the heat of struggles and injustices, we have a hard time understanding how in the world it can work for our good. And yet, God's word says it does. There are times when the thing we pray for, the passionate prayer we articulate, the fasting and calling others to agree with us, doesn't seem to work. It doesn't seem to bring about the desired results.

> **Word Truth**
>
> The words **all things** in the Hebrew is *pas,* and it means **individually, each, every, any, all, the whole, everyone, all things, everything.**

My mother's best friend had cancer 30 years ago. She was like family. She was so precious. God chose me to walk with her through the most trying part of her journey. She said that the Lord told her that her sickness was not unto death. Who was I to question that? So I did what I had been taught as a child that you do to get God's attention. *I began fasting.* I fasted nine days with no food, only water. I stayed with her in the hospital round the clock. I prayed, interceding for her healing, and I believed God would touch her body and heal her. One night she was in so much pain, she looked at me and said, "***Sharon, please touch God for me.***" I dropped to the floor brokenhearted and cried out to God asking Him for mercy. I saw how *powerless* I was for the first time in my life. *It was devastating.* During all those days of fasting and prayer, I just knew God would heal her. At a place of surrender, I prayed *"Father, if You're not going to heal her, please just take the pain away",* and you know what? *She fell asleep. No pain.* The next day she died peacefully, but **WHY?** ***Why didn't He heal her?*** I did everything I thought I was supposed to do to change God's mind, but it didn't work. That experience shook my whole belief system! My heart was broken and confused. I know that God has a divine will and purpose. He is sovereign, *but that is so hard to grasp when there is such pain and especially when you've done what you were taught would touch His heart.* God was teaching me something very valuable I needed to know. I didn't exactly know what, but I was open to hear and learn. I embraced the reality that God is in charge, and even though I don't know why, I know my Father. I know He knows best though it may not feel like it at the time. I trust Him, period!

PRAYER

God, I know You understand my heart, and thank You for not condemning me when my prayers aren't answered the way I feel they should have been. Though I don't understand Your ways, I love You, and I trust Your purpose in all things. Let me continue to be Your hope for those who are hurting. And I ask You to comfort with Your peace the one who is dealing with the **why.** Only You can do that, Father. Amen.

REFLECTION

Are you asking *why* today? Write down those things that you question. Today, can you trust God with the reason to the *why?*

Comfort

"Blessed be the God and Father of our Lord Jesus Christ, the Father of mercies and God of all comfort, who comforts us in all our tribulation, that we may be able to comfort those who are in any trouble, with the comfort with which we ourselves are comforted by God."
II Corinthians 1:3, 4

Several years ago I was caring for a friend with cancer. My son Justin was a small child. I was asked to stay with her a few nights, so Justin stayed with my parents. Upon my return home, as I got into the car, I noticed Justin was very lethargic. I held him in my lap, and he was comforted. I had not been told that he had been taken to the hospital and that his little body had a high fever and every joint swelled twice their size. He looked bruised on his joints and back. I hadn't been told that he had been tested for Leukemia. God had called me away to care for one of His children, and now I come home, and my baby is very ill. This was not right! I took him into my arms, and I began to pray and cry out to God. I began to pray in the spirit with groaning only God could understand, and I asked Him to heal my son. His fever immediately broke, and by the next day, all the swelling had gone down. God touched his little body and healed him. I was comforted. I felt so fortunate and blessed!

> **Word Truth**
> The word **comfort**, comes from the Greek word ***paraklesis***, and it means **a**

> **calling near, encouragement, comfort, refreshment, and consolation.**
>
> The word **know**, comes from the Greek word ***ginsoko***, and it means **to know, understand, perceive, and have knowledge of.**

Our nation, in the past few years, has experienced more natural disasters, human disasters such as the bombing at the Boston Marathon, shootings at schools and theaters, that hit the headlines with a fury. So many have suffered so much loss and pain, and it seems that there is little solace.

Here we go again to the question of why? Why did God allow these things to happen? Why did God allow Justin to become ill and heal him and not heal my friend? I have discovered that it is best to tell the truth in all circumstances and the truth is ... **I DON'T KNOW WHY.** I have discovered that I don't have to know why, I don't have to know the answers, and that's okay. I don't have to understand. Does that take away the pain of sorrow? NO, but I do find comfort in trusting God with the unknown.

When you are in deep pain, it is difficult to believe that God loves you and that He is mindful of where you are and what you are going through. But He is. There are no words eloquent enough to express God's love for you. The most expressive way He has shown His love is through Jesus, His only precious Son.

> *"Blessed be the God and Father of our Lord Jesus Christ, the Father of mercies and God of all comfort."*
> *II Corinthians 1:3*

I **know** that God cares about everything that concerns you and me. I **know** His Word is truth, and that it works.

I **know** He is sovereign. I **know** He will comfort us if we will trust Him. Perhaps, one day we will know the answer, or perhaps we won't. Regardless, it is when we trust Him we are comforted. We are comforted by God to comfort one another, to be tender-hearted and compassionate towards one another.

PRAYER

Holy Spirit, touch the one reading this prayer today who is hurting, wondering why. I ask You, Father, to bring Your peace to Your child's mind. You are the Healer of broken hearts. You do mend every shattered dream. Today, comfort them. Let Your peace fill their mind right now. Thank You, Father. We don't have to know why. We know that You know and that's enough. Amen.

REFLECTION

You may be hurting today, and you may be asking WHY. I want to challenge you to do something today. Embrace your lack of having full knowledge of all things and focus on the One who does, Jesus. I know it's so hard to grasp, but He sees beyond what we see and know. Trust that. Write down those things that are causing you pain. Who can you turn to who will truly comfort you in your pain?

_____

_____

No Negotiating

"So take a new grip with your tired hands, stand firm on your shaky legs and mark out a straight, smooth path for your feet so that those who follow you, though weak and lame will not fall and hurt themselves, but become strong." Hebrews 12:12, 13

When the enemy of our country attacked the Twin Towers in New York, the news reporters asked President Bush this question, "Will you sit down and confer with the Taliban?" And President Bush replied, **"THERE WILL BE NO NEGOTIATIONS!"**

> **Word Truth**
> Let's look at the word **negotiate**. It means to **bargain, settle, arbitrate, confer, dicker, compromise.**

You may have your own opinion of President Bush, but I like that statement. **No negotiating with the enemy**!

That is how we are to be when we face evil and deal with problems that are evil that would cause us to fear or pull us down. **WE MUST BE STRONG IN THE LORD AND THE POWER OF HIS MIGHT. WE MUST TAKE OUR STANCE AGAINST IT. NO NEGOTIATING!**

There is one thing we must understand ... there is a real enemy of our souls. His name is Satan, Lucifer, the Devil. He hates you and wants to destroy you and everybody you love. He is a tormenter. He will cause you to worry and fret over the **'what ifs'**.

What if ... I lose my house?
What if ... I lose my job?
What if ... I have to go bankrupt?
What if ... my companion leaves me?
What if ... I lose my health?

Well, **what if?** There are people every day who take their lives because of fear of the **'what ifs'**? But **we don't have to do that because we have God** who will help us and lead us **IF** any of these things happen. I know. I've experienced some of them myself, and yes, they shake your world. That is when the enemy will come to your mind with accusations and torment. It is in that time that you cannot negotiate with him. He is a liar! He will attack your mind when you are the weakest. But the Word says, *"When I am weak, He (God) is my strength."* Get a grip and stand firm on truth. You win!

"...God is our refuge and strength a very present help in trouble." Psalms 46:1

PRAYER
Father, You thoroughly know us. We are human and sometimes weak. We deal with emotions of the **'what ifs'.** We have to face them and try to prepare. Help us to recognize when things move beyond concern to fear, that is when the enemy strikes to bring us down. **He has no more power than we give him.** If we have given him power to bring about fear, then **right now, in the name of Jesus, we take that power back!** For we know that You are able to take care of everything that concerns us. We will **NOT** negotiate with

the enemy or give him another millisecond of our good brain time. Help us to look at the situation head on, ask You for wisdom to make the decisions we have to make, and push forward in Jesus Name. Amen.

REFLECTION

What are the *"what ifs"* you are dealing with? Have you been negotiating with something that is pulling you away from truth? If so, what?

_____
_____
_____
_____
_____
_____
_____

Thanks

"O give thanks unto the Lord, for He is good, for His mercy endures forever." Psalms 136:1

Have you noticed how unthankful this generation is? It seems as though they haven't been taught to be appreciative or thankful. And the generation coming up is following pursuit. It is so important to teach our children how to be appreciative, courteous and to say thank you when something is done, said or given to them that is good.

> **Word Truth** — The word **thanks** comes from the Hebrew word *yadah*. It means **to give thanks, laud, praise, confess the name of God, and thankful.**

Thanks is a very common word, but, oh, it is so powerful. It has the *power to change lives, to change circumstances, the power to turn hurt feelings into healing, pain into joy, disappointments into new beginnings*! This one word can bring a smile where there is sorrow. Thanks can comfort and bring peace. It is even able to bring a satisfaction where there has been question of appreciation. **THANKS** is a powerful word!

Doesn't it make you feel good when your child thanks you for something done or given to them? Or better yet, when they thank you for being their mom or dad? Wow, that really touches your heart. When a friend thanks you for being their friend, your companion thanks you for loving them, doesn't that make you feel good? Sure it does. We all love to be appreciated.

God's mercies are renewed for us everyday. That is so wonderful! He is longsuffering, never giving up on us. *Oh my goodness ... that is such a glorious thing to be thankful for.* God loves it when we love Him. He loves our affection and appreciation for His faithfulness, just for being who His is. He loves to hear us just say **thanks**. Have you thanked Him today for His goodness to you? Have you thanked Him today that you can breathe and walk, talk, think, and reason? Why not just do it right now.

Today, just take a moment to *thank* someone for their love, their kindness, maybe for just being who they are. Just take the time to say **thanks**. You really could make someone's day. And, I know **we make the heart of God happy when we say** *thanks*.

PRAYER

God, thank You for all You do for me. Thank You for water to drink, food to eat, and clothes to wear. Thank You for a roof over my head, a bed to sleep. Thank You for running water, hot and cold. Thank You for transportation, precious friends whom I love dearly. Thank You for my family I have been so blessed with. Thank You, most of all, for loving me so much, that You came to rescue me from hell. Thank You for giving me the hope of eternal life. I thank You, Father. I thank You, Jesus. I thank You, Holy Spirit for touching my life, guiding me in Your ways. I love You. Amen.

REFLECTION
What are you thankful for today?

_____

_____

_____

_____

_____

_____

_____

Enough's Enough

"Come now, and we will make a peace treaty, you and I, and we will live by its terms." Genesis 31:44

This is the most wonderful story of two men feuding and how they came to a place of peace. It is about Jacob and Laban. Jacob was a good man who loved the God of Abraham. Laban, on the other hand, was an idolater, liar, hard task master, and a cruel father, looking out for number one. He used people and never admitted to wrong doing. **Have you ever known anyone manipulative and self-serving?** That was Laban. Jacob worked for Laban so that he could marry Rachel, one of Laban's daughters. At the end of seven years, Laban lied and gave him Leah instead. So, Jacob worked another seven years for Rachel. Altogether he worked 20 years for Laban. *One day an angel appeared to Jacob and said, "It's time to go back home."* **Enough's, enough!** God said it was enough. It was time to make a truce. Laban had done Jacob wrong, but it was time to bring an end to it. Laban realized he was losing his daughters and grandchildren, and he knew he needed to make peace. So Jacob took a stone and set it up as a memorial, and he told his servants to pile up stones. Then Jacob and Laban sat between them and had a meal. The rocks were a witness of the covenant between them. In Hebrew, it was called ***edah,*** which means **something that bears witness or something that testifies of.** They brought an end to their bad relationship.

Relationships, whether it be with family, friends,

employees or employers, can be unpleasant, devastating, overwhelming and bring us pain. They literally can take away our peace of mind, **until someone declares a truce.**

It's okay to air your differences, but be civil if you can. There are times when you have to bring things to an end ... *wind it up*! When you realize it must be done for your peace of mind, that knowledge alone can empower your life. Be *wise* in how you handle your affairs. Use discretion and good judgment. Sometimes to do that, we have to seek the wisdom of those who have more knowledge into things we question or lack knowledge about.

There are five things you can do to pursue healing, if not for anyone else, then for yourself, but you must mean it. These words carry tremendous power when sincerely spoken.

I'm sorry
I was wrong
Forgive me
I love you
Thank you

Many times we are afraid to reach out again, afraid that we will be taken advantage of or rejected. We look at the track record, and it makes us gun shy. We doubt the sincerity. Only you know when you have reached the end of yourself and when you must proclaim **PEACE**. They may reject your efforts, but what matters is that you try. Then you can let go and move forward. Don't throw the stone at them (*though you may feel like it*). Give it to them as a sign of sincerity, a stone of forgiveness.

– *Adapted from a message by Loranie Daniel.*

PRAYER

Father, it is difficult sometimes to forgive and especially when it isn't our fault. It makes it hard to ask forgiveness of something when we are not guilty. Nevertheless, help us to forgive and make peace. Life is too short to hold a grudge. And, besides that, Your Word says *'if we don't forgive, we won't be forgiven by You'*. Help us to forgive. Help us to take the first step. *Though we may have to disconnect, we won't discount them.* In Your Name, Amen.

REFLECTION

Who do you need to forgive? Have you been manipulative to get your way? Do you need to disconnect from someone? What can you do to make peace?

_____

_____

_____

_____

_____

_____

_____

His Workmanship

"For we are his workmanship, created in Christ Jesus unto good works, which God has before ordained that we should walk in them." Ephesians 2:10

Word Truth

The word **workmanship** from the Greek is *poiema*. It's where we get our word *poem*. It means you are **God's achievement, His creation, His accomplishment, His masterpiece.**

WOW! You are somebody special! Look at what David is inspired to write in the Psalms.

"You made all the delicate, inner parts of my body and knit me together in my mother's womb. Thank you for making me so wonderfully complex! Your workmanship is marvelous – and how well I know it. You watched me as I was being formed in utter seclusion, as I was woven together in the dark of the womb. You saw me before I was born. Every day of my life was recorded in your book. Every moment was laid out before a single day had passed. How precious are your thoughts about me, O God! They are innumerable! I can't even count them; they outnumber the grains of sand! And when I wake up in the morning, you are still with me!" Psalms 139:13-18

Oh my goodness! **Do you see how much God loves you?** You may not feel like He loves you. You may be struggling today, but I am telling you that He loves you with an everlasting love. **You are His treasure, His masterpiece.** Do you really know what that means? Here's how Webster defines it: *a work done with extraordinary skill; especially a supreme intellectual or artistic achievement.* **THAT'S YOU!**

How you feel about yourself doesn't nullify the fact that God took great care in creating you, everything about you. So, straighten up and ACT like it!

When someone or something tries to make you feel bad, apply what Loraine Daniel called the **"2-D"** method ... ***Don't discount them, but disconnect.*** You may not be able to disconnect from them permanently, but you can for awhile. Walk away and regroup. Remember who you are. Don't give away your power. You are God's kid!

PRAYER
Father, when I think about how You created me with such care, it blows me away! I see Your loving hand in every part of me. Thank You for seeing me complete and whole. Thank You because You've seen my beginning and what I will be in the end ... perfected in You. Can't wait! Help me share Your love to others. I love You. Amen.

REFLECTION

Do you know how much God loves you? What does it mean to be God's "workmanship?"

_____

_____

_____

_____

_____

_____

_____

Train Your Senses

"Train your senses so that you will be able to discern good from evil." Hebrews 5:14

Someone told me a story about a guy who went to church every Sunday. The Pastor would make his altar call, and this guy would go up every Sunday. And every time he went forward kneeling to pray, he would begin to cry and say, "**O God, clean the cob webs out of my mind. OOOOOHHHHHH God, clean the cob webs out of my mind.**" One day when he prayed that prayer, the Pastor walked by and said, "**GOD, KILL THE SPIDER.**"

God gives us enough common sense to do some things ourselves. **The word senses is an organ of perception.** What encompasses our organ of perception? It is our *sight, hearing, touch, smell, taste* and our *mind*. You know, we really do have the habit of wanting God to do things that He's just not going to do. **He's not going to turn off a bad movie that causes you to lust. He's not going to stop you from cussing. He's not going to make you close that bad magazine. He's not going to make you have a good attitude. He's not going to make you forgive. He's not going to make you stop gossiping. He's not going to make you stop hating. He's not going to force you to be good. He's not going to stop you from lying.** Catch my drift? **WE** are responsible for our actions and choices. **We train our senses when we study God's Word and put it into practice.** In doing so, we fortify our minds to know how to come against **evil**, *those things that* *would pull us away from what is good, healthy and pleasing to God.*

> **Word Truth**
>
> The word **senses** comes from the Greek word *aistheterion,* and it means **faculty of the mind for perceiving, understanding, and judging.**

If you are pursuing God and renewing your mind with His Word, He will strengthen you in every challenging situation you face. He has blessed us with an incredible gift … **our minds**, and with that mind we choose to do what is **right** or we choose what is **wrong**. We choose to **love** or to **hate**. We choose to be **mad** or **glad**. We choose to be **bitter** or **sweet**. We choose to be **kind** or **hateful**. We choose to be a **victim** or a **victor**. **KILL THE SPIDER!**

"Do not be overcome by evil, but overcome evil with good." Romans 12:21

PRAYER

Father, there is constant conflict that I deal with in my mind, right and wrong, good and evil. I thank You for the power of Your Word and the mental ability to reason and make right choices that will please You and be good for me and those around me. Today, I choose to do what is right, I choose to think what is right, and in doing so, You've promised to help me. You are so precious to me. I love You. Amen.

REFLECTION

What's it going to be today? What do you want God to do that He has given you the ability to do yourself? What do you need to do to discipline your mind and life?

God's Will

"And so, dear brothers and sisters, I plead with you to give your bodies to God. Let them be a living and holy sacrifice – the kind He will accept. When you think of what He has done for you, is this too much to ask? Don't copy the behavior and customs of this world, but let God transform you into a new person by changing the way you think. Then you will know what God wants you to do, and you will know how good and pleasing His will really is."
Romans 12:1, 2

One of the most frequent questions that Christians ask is **"What's God's will for my life?"** The Scripture above really gives us direction as to finding God's will. God uses ordinary people to accomplish extraordinary things! Just ordinary people like you and me. Here is another good question … **"How do I find God's will for my life?" First, dedicate your life to God.** Offer yourself, every part of you. Offer Him your talents and gifts, your time, finances, and relationships. **Second, communicate with God (pray).** You have to spend time alone with God, quiet time without distractions to hear Him speak, not just every now and then, but on a daily basis. **Third, evaluate yourself and your abilities.**

II Corinthians 13:5 says "Examine and evaluate your own selves to see whether you are holding to your faith and showing the proper fruits of it."

God has given us gifts according to our own individual

abilities. Ask yourself these two questions:

What am I good at?
What do I love to do?

Then, ask yourself how God can use these gifts for His Kingdom. Not everybody can sing. Not everyone can teach. Not everyone has a desire to be a missionary or pastor. But, **everybody has something they can use to bring glory to God.** Do you like to cook, sew, build, clean, read? Do you enjoy math, yard work? **What do you enjoy doing?** You may be a great organizer. Do you enjoy writing?

Now you may be thinking "How can God use that"? Well, here are a few ways. There are people who are too ill to fix their meal, but you can! There are plenty of families and seniors who don't have enough blankets or quilts, and you can sew. There are widows and seniors who need repairs on their homes. Someone ill or elderly can't clean their house, but you can. Children love for someone to read to them. You can do that at a church or school program or create a kids reading club. Kids need lots of help in math. People need help with their taxes and can't afford to pay for that help. *Do you see what I am getting at?* Writing a note of encouragement to someone means so much. God uses what we have been already given. **When we do those things as unto Him, it brings great fulfillment, and you have found His will.**

PRAYER

Father, I give You all of me. Help me to reach out to others in Your love with what I have been given. Thank You, Amen.

REFLECTION

The whole purpose of your salvation was not just to go to heaven. **No! We are saved to serve. We are saved to love and help others. We are saved to lead others to Jesus by the way we live. This is the will of God for us.** Are you obeying His will?

Hope Deferred

"Hope deferred (put off) makes the heart (mind) sick, but when the desire comes, it is a tree of life."
Proverbs 13:12

Today I have given thought to a phone call I received from my mother. A teenage boy in the city where she lives had committed suicide. My heart ached for the parents at this devastating news.

Why would one so young feel so hopeless? A break up of a girlfriend, bad grades, unpopular, bullied? My heart aches, but something came to my mind today about life. You know truthfully, life is difficult even with Jesus. I began to imagine life without Him.

When Adam and Eve sinned, it threw everything into chaos. Hopelessness came into fruition. Life became very hard. Down through the years up until Jesus came, man had to try to obey the law which was pretty impossible to do. If the sacrifices weren't accepted by God, you were a goner! I want you to think about something here. **Do you realize that they did not have something we have access to?** They had to try to please God on their own. When Jesus came and fulfilled the law, meaning that He followed all tenants of it without sin, and when He had completed His ministry, was crucified, died and was resurrected and ascended back to heaven, **He left us something**. He left us **His Holy Spirit** to **LIVE IN US**! Oh, how I hope you get this. We have the Spirit of God in us when we accept Jesus into our lives as our Savior! We have the very one who raised Him from the dead living in us! **THIS GIVES US HOPE! THIS GIVES US STRENGTH TO ENDURE** the test, the bad news, sickness, sorrow, loss. We have **His grace** that is sufficient to get us through every hopeless situation if we call on Him! Praise God! He didn't leave us alone, but is with us and lives in us!

> **Word Truth**
>
> **Hope** comes from the Hebrew word *towcheleth*, and it means **expectation**.
>
> **Deferred** comes from the Hebrew word *mashak*, and it means **put off, postpone, prolong**.

Suicide has become the 4th largest killer of our children ages 10 – 14. You read that right, ages 10 – 14. **WHY?** Some are bullied and made fun of. They are hearing there is no hope for the future every time you turn on the TV or radio. They are hearing their parents talking about it. They see them frightened, and they are feeling there is no hope! If you are a parent reading this today, I want to encourage you to turn the news off once in a while. Your children are watching for your reaction. If we show fear, they will fear and become insecure. **Hope put off or prolonged produces hopelessness. We must give hope.** Be aware of your conversation around your children. What are you showing them? What are you speaking? Is it hope? **Jesus told us that in this world we would have trouble, but He also said, "Be of good cheer, I have overcome the world".** What exactly does that mean? It means that **WE ARE NOT ALONE! WE HAVE HIS HOLY SPIRIT LIVING IN US!** God knows what is going on economically. God is aware of it all, and He is with us to help us through it.

PRAYER

Father, help me to be sensitive to our children. Help me to discern when they are in trouble and give me the wisdom to help them. Help me to discipline my conversation. Help me to guard my mind and help me to give hope in hopeless situations. In the name of Your Son, Jesus. Amen.

REFLECTION

Do you feel alone? What is causing that emotion? Do you recognize the Holy Spirit is here to help you? Do you really realize God lives in you? How does that make you feel?

Make It Easy On Yourself

"For my yoke is easy and my burden is light."
Matthew 11:30

Have you ever wondered exactly what that Scripture means? I will define four of the key words in that verse for you.

> **Word Truth**
>
> The word **yoke** comes from the Greek word *zygos*, and it is used as a metaphor, **used of any burden or bondage. It is a tool used for balance.**
>
> The word **easy** comes from the Greek word *chrestos*, and it means **fit for use, useful, more pleasant.**
>
> The word **burden** comes from the Greek word *phortion*, and it means **burden, load, oppression.** And lastly, the word **light** comes from the Greek word *elaphros*, and it means **light in weight, quick, agile.**

Here is a word picture to really open up your understanding of this scripture. Have you ever seen two oxen with yokes around their shoulders? You usually see them in third world countries out plowing rough, dry terrain. They yoke up a young ox with an old ox. That's called **coupling**, and they do that because the older one knows the terrain. Now, sometimes you will notice the younger one pulling against the old ox. He's wanting to go his own way, do his own thing. This is good! The older ox is more stubborn, and he keeps pulling the younger one back on the path. Are you beginning to get the picture?

Jesus said, **"My yoke is easy and my burden is light"**. I like to say it like this ... **when we couple up with Jesus, it is useful and the burden** (the thing that causes you oppression or pulls you down) **becomes lighter**. You want to know why? ***It's because Jesus knows the terrain*****. He knows where the pitfalls are, He understands sorrow, disappointment, and pain. He's been there, and He has made the path straight!** ***We just need to follow His lead*****!**

Sometimes our bad days are bad simply because we are trying to fix things ourselves. We go here and there searching for answers instead of yielding to Jesus, taking them to Him in prayer. Sometimes we are pulling against His lead, and life is so heavy when we do that. If we would just yield our will, our problems to Him, we could handle life so much better.

I read a story about a man by the name of Joseph Scrivens. Joseph's fiancé died the night before they were to be married. He yielded his broken heart to Jesus in prayer and in deep sorrow. It wasn't long after that his mother became ill, and he wrote her a letter and enclosed the lines of a poem he had written. This poem is now a song ... **"What A Friend We Have In Jesus."** Read what he expresses in these lines of the first verse and chorus.

What a friend we have in Jesus, All our sins and griefs to bear
What a privilege to carry, everything to God in prayer.
Oh what grief we often forfeit, Oh what needless pain we bear
All because we do not carry, everything to God in prayer.

PRAYER

Father, why is it that I think I can fix it all? Why do I wait until life is so heavy to yoke up with You? I don't want to do that! I want to yield to You all of those things that weigh me down. You do know the terrain, and I trust Your lead. Help me to quickly get in line. Then You will give me wisdom and with You, all things will work together for my good. Help me to *make it easy on myself.* I love You, Jesus. Amen.

REFLECTION

Are you carrying something too heavy for you to carry? Have you taken it to the Lord in prayer? Have you yoked up (coupled up) with Jesus?

_____
_____
_____
_____
_____
_____
_____

Enough Faith

"As they approached Jericho, a blind beggar was sitting beside the road. When he heard the noise of a crowd going past, he asked what was happening. They told him that Jesus of Nazareth was going by. So he began shouting, "Jesus, Son of David, have mercy on me!" The crowds ahead of Jesus tried to hush the man, but he only shouted louder, "Son of David, have mercy on me!" When Jesus heard him, he stopped and ordered that the man be brought to him. Then Jesus asked the man, "What do you want me to do for you?" "Lord," he pleaded, "I want to see!" And Jesus said, "All right, you can see! Your faith has healed you. Instantly the man could see, and he followed Jesus, praising God. And all who saw it praised God too."
Luke 18:35-43

Jesus could see this man was blind, and yet, he asked him what he wanted Him to do. He wanted the blind man to identify his need.

Our measure of faith will be according to our need. If you need a little faith, you will have a little faith. If you need great faith, you will have great faith. We have all been given the same measure of faith. In essence, Jesus was saying, **"You have enough faith, be healed."**

Do you know what I love about this story? I love the ***persistence*** of the blind man. The crowd tried to shut him up, but they couldn't. The more they tried, the louder he got! Evidently, he had heard about this Jesus who opened deaf ears, raised the dead, healed the blind, and he wasn't about to let Him pass by without giving it his best shot, and so he yelled to the top of his voice! **"Jesus, Son of David, have mercy on me!"** And it got Jesus' attention. Interestingly, Jesus knew this man was blind and even knew his heart's desire to see, but He asked him anyhow. **"What do you want me to do?"** The man was a beggar. He could have asked for money, but that would have only been a temporary fix. What he needed was his sight and then he could work and take care of himself and, perhaps a family! So Jesus gave him his sight. Then, he rejoiced and praised God!

Let's look at something here. The blind man called Jesus **'Son of David'**, a title for the **Messiah**. *This means that he understood Jesus to be the long-awaited Messiah. Isn't it interesting that a poor blind beggar could **see** that Jesus was the Messiah, while the religious leaders who visibly saw His miracles were **blinded** to His identity and refused to recognize Him as the Messiah.*

In this story we see a **problem** ... a blind man. We see **provision** ... Jesus. And we see the **promise** ... salvation and healing. It is in Jesus! We have been given **enough faith** in Jesus to meet our needs.

PRAYER

Father, I believe in Your Son, Jesus Messiah, to meet my need. Provision was made at Calvary and I hold to the promise of Your Word that You will _____ (your need) in Your time, Your way, for my good. However You do it, I accept as Your will. Thank You, Jesus. Amen.

REFLECTION

What is your need today? Identify it and tell it to Him. Persevere, don't give up! And believe Him to meet that need. Act upon the faith that you have ... it's enough faith ... and see what God will do.

Serve

"Each one should use whatever gift he has received to serve others, faithfully administering God's grace in its various forms." 1 Peter 4:10

What did Jesus do while He was on this earth? Let's take a moment to look at His short life. He was Messiah, born in a stable. He grew in the wisdom of God. Though He was Messiah, He **humbled** himself to be baptized by John the Baptist. He was led out to the desert, and there He fasted 40 days and nights. Satan tempted Him in all ways that we are tempted, and yet **He didn't sin.** He taught and fed multitudes of people, healing all who were sick, raising the dead. He called fishermen, tax collectors, thieves to be His **disciples.** He preached a message of **selflessness** to a selfish humanity. He preached **love your enemies, bless** those who curse you, be **merciful,** be **pure** in your minds, **hate evil** and **love what is good**, and when you are persecuted … **rejoice!** He taught us to **forgive** as we have been forgiven by God. He showed us **mercy.** He taught us to **pray,** to be **generous** givers. He taught us to put **God first,** and He showed us how to do that by how He lived. He taught us to **seek God's help** and **guidance**, to ask for **wisdom,** to be **compassionate** and **kind,** to be **thankful.** He told us to pursue **peace.** He showed us how to **witness** about God's **love** to others. He taught us what it means to **sacrifice.** He taught us what **grace** is. His life exemplified **obedience** to God. He spoke **hope** and **life!** He showed us the importance of **work** and **rest.** He taught us to be **discerning** of the methods of the devil who is always trying to destroy our joy, hope and souls. He taught us how to be **victorious** over the enemy, the devil. He really showed us what **family** is ... **loyalty, trust, integrity** and **love**. He showed us **the way** to God, and He told us how to obtain **eternal life**. He did all of this in 33 short years!

> **Word Truth**
>
> The Greek word for **serve** is *diakoneo,* and it means **to serve, wait upon, minister to one, to take care of.**

Jesus came to show us how to please God by serving others. The Bible says that **"Jesus came not to be served, but to serve."** Sometimes I think we have life all wrong. We spend the majority of our time and efforts on **things** here, tangible on this earth. And yet, the most important things we often ignore are those things that have eternal value. Why is it that we put those things on the back burner when in all reality, those are the **things** that really matter? After all, Scripture says that the things here on earth that we work so hard to obtain will rot away, turn to dust, moths will eat, worms will destroy. Do we really believe in eternal life? Do we really believe Jesus is the Son of God? Statistics say that 60% of those who claim to be Christians don't believe Jesus is the only way to God. That's scary. What do you believe? Where are your priorities? Where are your treasures? Maybe it's time to **RE-THINK** life ... true life. Are you willing to serve?

PRAYER

Father, I do realize that life here on earth is short no matter how long one lives. We work so hard to obtain things here, when most of the time, if truth be known, we neglect what is truly important, those things that are eternal. Help me to be like Jesus. I want to love like Him, to serve like Him. To show grace and mercy towards others as You desire me to do. Help me to prioritize my life here to bless You and build Your Kingdom. I ask these things in the Name of Your Son, Jesus. Amen.

REFLECTION
Do you believe Jesus is the only way to God? Are you willing to really serve like Jesus?

_____
_____
_____
_____
_____
_____

God With Skin On Him

"How precious is your unfailing love, O God!
All humanity finds shelter in the shadow of your wings."
Psalms 36:7

There was a terrible storm one night, with crashing and thunder resounding in the sky. It was so loud that the house would vibrate ever time the lightning struck the earth. A little boy, whom we will call Tommy, cried out to his mother, "Mama, Mama, I'm scared" as he lay in bed that night. The mama called back, "It will be okay, Tommy." A few minutes went by and lightning crashed the earth again. "Mama, Mama, I'm scared," Tommy cried out. "It's going to be okay Tommy. God is with us." A few minutes passed by again the struck the earth, the thunder roared. "Mama, Mama, I'm really scared". About that time his Mama became a little aggravated and said, "Tommy, you are going to be fine. I told you. God is with us." Tommy said, "Maaaaaama, Maaaama, I know God is with us, but what I need right now is God with skin on Him!"

Have you ever needed God with skin on him? You just needed someone to put their arms around you and hold you real close and everything would be okay. Have you ever needed to hear a kind word spoken that would comfort your heart? I can remember holding my son, Justin, many times when he was a little boy frightened, and he would immediately be comforted. There is a whole world that is scared, and they need **God with skin on Him**. They are insecure, frightened about the future. You and I have been given the most amazing gift. We are called to be God with skin on Him. In our actions, our attitudes, our time, and our lives we are called to **love one another as God has loved us.**

"Dear friends, let us continue to love one another, for love comes from God. Anyone who loves is born of God and knows God. But anyone who does not love does not know God – for God is love. God showed how much he loved us by sending his only Son into the world so that we might have eternal life through him. This is real love. It is not that we loved God but that he loved us and sent his Son as a sacrifice to take away our sins. Dear Friends, since God loved us that much, we surely ought to love each other. No one has ever seen God. But if we love each other, God lives in us, and his loved has been brought to full expression through us." I John 4:7-12

We have the awesome opportunity to be an example of God's love to one another. God never turns a deaf ear to our cries, nor should we when someone needs help. There is such tremendous power in our words. Our words can comfort a broken heart. Our words can bring hope in a hopeless situation. Our hands can bring healing through a tender touch on the shoulder. Our arms can strengthen one who feels weak. That's what Jesus would do, and that is what we are called to do.

PRAYER

The storms of life are raging. Uncertainty is all around us, but You, O Lord, have given us the awesome privilege to represent who You are to others. We are called to love others as You have loved us. Help us get beyond our own agendas and touch those who are hurting today with Your love. Help us be 'God with skin on him.' Amen.

REFLECTION
How can you be 'God with skin on him' to someone today?

I Will Always Be Here For You

"Teach these new disciples to obey all the commands I have given you. And be sure of this: I am with you always, even to the end of the age." Matthew 28:20

I read a story about a little boy in another country that was trapped under the debris of a school that had collapsed when an earthquake hit the area where he lived. The rescue workers were digging through the rubble to find survivors. After a few hours of pulling body after body from the rubble, they gave up hope of finding anyone else alive. They called off the search.

This young boy's father ran past the barricade and started searching through the rubble for his son. Everyone tried to convince him that his son was dead and that it was useless to keep searching. The father ignored all those around him and **kept digging and searching**. Hours went by, and then night fell, but he kept searching. The police tried to get him to go home, but **the father refused**. One day went by, then two days, and on the third day, as he was digging, **he heard something**. He could hear a faint voice saying, **"Hold on, my dad is coming. Hold on, my dad will find us."** As the man broke through the rubble, he heard his son say, **"Dad, is that you?"** The father replied, **"Yes son, it's me!"** The son said, **"Dad, I told them that you would come for us and that you would find us."**

What kept those children alive? **HOPE!** What gave that little boy hope? He remembered his dad's words to him ... **"Son, I WILL ALWAYS BE HERE FOR YOU."** The words of that father gave his son hope to survive.

There are many things in life that you can't count on ... many things in life that are uncertain. Here is one thing that is certain ... **God is with you all the time, whether you feel it or not.** Regardless of what happens, you and I don't have to go through it alone. Our Father is there for us. **He is there for you.**

"Don't worry, because I AM WITH YOU. Don't be afraid, because I AM YOUR GOD. I WILL MAKE YOU STRONG AND WILL HELP YOU; I WILL SUPPORT YOU with My right hand that saves you." Isaiah 41:10

PRAYER

"Lord, remember my suffering and my misery, my sorrow and trouble. Please remember me and think about me. But I have hope when I think of this. The Lord's love never ends; His mercies never stop. They are new every morning; Lord, your loyalty is great. I say to myself, The Lord is mine, SO I HOPE IN HIM." *Lamentations 3:19-24.* Thank You for the words of Jesus ... "I will never leave you, I will never forsake you. I am with you always even unto the end of the age". Thank You.

REFLECTION

Do you have that childlike faith knowing that "God Will Always Be There For You?" Do you believe it?

_____
_____
_____
_____
_____
_____
_____

Love God Where You Are

"He shall sit as a refiner and purifier of silver; and he shall purify the sons of Levi and purge them as gold and silver, that they may offer unto the Lord an offering in righteousness." Malachi 3:3

One day at a ladies Bible study, they were studying the book of Malachi. They were reading Malachi 3:3, and one of them questioned what the verse **"He shall sit as a refiner and purifier of silver"** meant. How did this describe the character and nature of God? So, one of the women volunteered to go to a silversmith and find out. She made an appointment with the silversmith not telling him why she wanted to watch him process the silver.

The day arrived for her to go to the silversmith's, and she watched as he held a piece of silver over the fire and let it heat up. **He explained that in refining silver, one needed to hold the silver in the middle of the fire where the flames were the hottest so as to burn away all the impurities.**

The woman thought about God **holding us in such a hot spot**. Then she thought again about that verse **"He sits as a refiner and purifier of silver"**, and she asked the silversmith **if it was true that he had to sit there in front of the fire the whole time the silver was being refined.** The man answered, "Yes." **He not only had to sit there holding the silver, but he had to keep his eyes on the silver the entire time it was in the fire.** IF the silver was left even one minute too long in the flames, it would be destroyed. The woman was silent for a moment, then she asked the silversmith one more question, **"How do you know when the silver is fully refined?** He smiled at her and answered, "Oh that's the easy part – **when I see my image reflected in it."** WOW!

You may feel as though you are in the middle of the fire. You feel like you can't take any more ... any more pressure, any more trouble, and any more losses! **You have been so confused.** You don't understand ... why is this taking so long? Why is God allowing this? Why doesn't He do something! Let's go back to the Scripture.

"He shall sit as a <u>refiner</u> and purifier of silver; and he shall purify the sons of Levi and purge them as gold and silver, that they may offer to the Lord an offering in <u>righteousness</u>."
Malachi 3:3

> **Refiner** comes from the Hebrew word *tsaraph,* and it means **to test, to prove true, purge away** (a metaphor).
> **Righteousness** comes from the Hebrew word *tedaquah,* and it means **to be right, just, salvation, and whole.**

I have to tell you the truth ... I have no idea as to why so many are struggling, why there are so many perplexed and puzzled, other than **God is holding us in the middle of the fire to perfect His love in us. His eyes are always on us and <u>He will not leave us there a minute too long</u>. It is a test of our faith. We will be held there right in the middle of the hot spot until He sees the reflection of His Son in us.**

PRAYER

Help me Father, to be still, to wait and trust You. Help me to not give up but to hold on to hope and love You where I am. Amen.

REFLECTION

Can you love God where you are?

Examine Yourself

"Examine me, O Lord, and prove me; try my reins and my heart." Psalm 26:2

What in the world does **'try my reins'** mean?

> **Word Truth**
>
> **Reins** comes from the Hebrew word *kilyah*, and it has two meanings. 1.) **kidney.** *(Well, hello ... try my kidneys? I don't think so.)* 2.) It also means **the inmost mind, as the seat of desires and affections.** Ah, now that makes sense.

Remember, the word **heart** comes from the word *leb*, and it means **the mind, intellect, the will, the seat of emotions, affections, desires, the inmost part of a person.** I love this!

One translator said that he felt the word **reins** was used because it was double. For example, when you put a bridle on a horse, it also has reins. Two leather straps to guide the horse. You can make it go right or left, back up or go forward, or make a complete circle.

We have what the Bible calls **a carnal mind** which is **naturally self-centered, self-serving.** Then, with that same mind, we can become **spiritual,** which means that we, because of Christ, are able to become **selfless, humble, and compassionate**, because with that spiritual mind, we **desire to serve God and others.**

*"To be carnally minded is death,
but to be spiritually minded is life and peace."*
Romans 8:6

You have the choice to go with death or life. You can be carnal and do your thing, which will take you away from God's virtue, power and safety, or you can become spiritual by accepting Christ into your life, reading His Word, and practice living it out. Aren't you amazed at God's love? He doesn't force you to do anything, but there are consequences that follow our choices, both good and bad. It's totally up to us! Do you see the reins? You have the choice to choose life or death.

The apostle Paul in II Corinthians wrote about what God taught him and what gave him power to live positively in Christ in the midst of fear, uncertainty, imprisonment, floggings, mocking, shipwrecked, and left for dead. I would say these were some kind of tests! He had the choice to hate God, to become bitter, but instead He loved God and was a passionate fanatic for Him! He said in *II Corinthians 13:4* that he was weak, but that Christ lived in him and gave him God's power. Isn't that what you want?

"Examine yourselves to see if your faith is really genuine. Test yourselves. If you cannot tell that Jesus Christ is among you, it means you have failed the test."
II Corinthians 13:5

PRAYER
Father, search me and know me, see if there is anything that is not pleasing to You. If there is, remove it, forgive me, and help me to live truth always before You and others. Hold my reins and lead me on the right path. Amen.

REFLECTION

As long as we live, we will be tested to see if our faith is true. And, it is important that we examine ourselves to keep our faith in check. If we see we have drifted away from God and we're flunking the test, we can come back and make things right through repentance. The world is waiting for us to live truth. Have you drifted away from truth?

_____
_____
_____
_____
_____
_____
_____
_____

Are You Ready?

> *"Jesus said to his disciples, 'The harvest is so great, but the workers are so few. So pray to the Lord who is in charge of the harvest; ask him to send out more workers for his fields.'"*
> Matthew 9:37, 38

When we have come through those tough times and our faith is intact, we are then able to help others. We are prepared to reach out. We are able to be a witness of God's faithfulness and trustworthiness by sharing what He has done for us. You must know who Jesus is and be convinced that He is the Son of God and that He came to show us the only way to God and that way is through Him.

It has been my desire to help you understand that it is only what we do for Christ that will last. To help you create a new way of thinking (not the norm) that the true treasures are what we do that has eternal value. It is investing our time, finances, and lives to help others, therefore sharing the love of God with them. It is realizing that though we hurt and are tested, if we are faithful to truth, we will come forth as pure gold, refined with the face of Jesus shining in us.

I know that life is tough, and at times, it is really unfair. But that's life! It really is just life. It's not because you are so bad or you've done something that you think God is punishing you for, life can just be unfair and full of injustices. That's just the truth and it doesn't matter how good you are or how much faith you have.

IS YOUR SOUL PREPPED? Have you made that total

surrender to His will? Are you ready to be a witness today? Are you ready to share what God has done for you to someone who is unchurched, who is lost and hurting? Share with someone who would give anything to know Jesus as you know Him? It is difficult to absorb, but there are thousands in our generation who only know God and Jesus as slang words. They know nothing about them at all. Here in America, a 'Christian nation', **there are thousands of people who do not know who Jesus is and what He came to do for them.** I pray God begins to break your heart for the lost ... those in your family who are lost, your neighbors, your friends. May you begin to weep for them until they are saved. Fortify your mind with God's Word and train yourself to be obedient to it.

PRAYER
Father, today I surrender all. I surrender what I hold dear – my dreams, my desires, my agenda – because more than anything in this world, I want my life to please You. I want to lay at Your feet souls who are searching for truth. O God, I really do want to be a witness by the way I live, because to some, I will be the only Bible they ever read. Lord, I know I am far from perfect, and I need Your help. Use me, Father, use my life for Your glory. Let me be a conduit of Your love to this hurting world around me. I ask this in Jesus' name. Amen.

REFLECTION

What have you learned from Soul Prep? How can you apply it? Will you tell people who Jesus is and what He came to do? Are you ready?

_____
_____
_____
_____
_____
_____
_____

Encouragement For Your Soul

"The Lord is my rock and my fortress and my deliverer; My God, my strength, in whom shall I fear? The Lord is the strength of my life; Of whom shall I be afraid?"
Psalm 27:1

"God is my strength and power, and He makes my way perfect."
2 Samuel 22:33

"Fear not, for I am with you; Be not dismayed, for I am your God. I will strengthen you, Yes, I will help you, I will uphold you with My righteous right hand."
Isaiah 41:10

*"The Lord will give strength to His people;
The Lord will bless His people with peace."
Psalm 29:11*

*"He gives power to the weak, And to those who have no might He increases strength. Even the youths shall faint and be weary, and the young men shall utterly fall. But those who wait on the Lord shall renew their strength: They shall mount up with wings like eagles, they shall run and not be weary, they shall walk and not faint."
Isaiah 20:29 -31*

*"Now if God so clothes the grass of the field, which today is, and tomorrow is thrown into the oven, will He not much more clothe you, O you of little faith?"
Matthew 6:30*

We appreciate hearing your questions and learning how you were affected by *Soul Prep*.

Living Hope
Attn: Sharon Boland
PO Box 2840
Cleveland, GA 30528

Send your comments or questions by email to
livinghope777@aol.com.